EDGE BOOKS

INFECTED!

SMALLPOX

HOW A POX CHANGED HISTORY

by Janie Havemeyer

raintree

a Capstone company — publishers for children

Raintree is an imprint of Capstone Global Library Limited, a company incorporated in England and Wales having its registered office at 264 Banbury Road, Oxford, OX2 7DY – Registered company number: 6695582

www.raintree.co.uk
myorders@raintree.co.uk

Text © Capstone Global Library Limited 2019
The moral rights of the proprietor have been asserted.

All rights reserved. No part of this publication may be reproduced in any form or by any means (including photocopying or storing it in any medium by electronic means and whether or not transiently or incidentally to some other use of this publication) without the written permission of the copyright owner, except in accordance with the provisions of the Copyright, Designs and Patents Act 1988 or under the terms of a licence issued by the Copyright Licensing Agency, Barnard's Inn, 86 Fetter Lane, London, EC4A 1EN (www.cla.co.uk). Applications for the copyright owner's written permission should be addressed to the publisher.

Edited by Maddie Spalding
Designed by Craig Hinton
Production by Ryan Gale
Originated by Capstone Global Library Ltd
Printed and bound in India

ISBN 978 1 4747 7537 3 (hardback)
23 22 21 20 19
10 9 8 7 6 5 4 3 2 1

ISBN 978 1 4747 7042 2 (paperback)
24 23 22 21 20
10 9 8 7 6 5 4 3 2 1

British Library Cataloguing in Publication Data
A full catalogue record for this book is available from the British Library.

Acknowledgements
We would like to thank the following for permission to reproduce photographs: Alamy: Marion Kaplan, 25, Trinity Mirror/Mirrorpix, 26; Defense Visual Information Distribution Service: Petty Officer 2nd Class Ashante Hammons, 28–29; Getty Images: Patrick Landmann/Getty Images News, 13; National Archives Catalog: Russell Lee, cover (people); Newscom: BSIP/Photoshot, 8, UPPA/Photoshot, 17; North Wind Picture Archives: 14; Shutterstock Images: chrisdorney, 21, Everett Historical, 7, 11, 19, 23, Everett-Art, 5, Kateryna Kon, cover (virus). Design elements: Shutterstock Images: ilolab.

Quote Sources

p. 4, Howard W. Haggard, *From Medicine Man to Doctor: The Story of the Science of Healing.* Mineola, N.Y.: Dover Publications, 2004; p. 20, Stefan Riedel, "Edward Jenner and the History of Smallpox and Vaccination." *Baylor University Medical Center,* January 2005

Every effort has been made to contact copyright holders of material reproduced in this book. Any omissions will be rectified in subsequent printings if notice is given to the publisher.

All the internet addresses (URLs) given in this book were valid at the time of going to press. However, due to the dynamic nature of the internet, some addresses may have changed, or sites may have changed or ceased to exist since publication. While the author and publisher regret any inconvenience this may cause readers, no responsibility for any such changes can be accepted by either the author or the publisher.

CONTENTS

CHAPTER 1

THE DEADLY POX

On 20 December 1694, Queen Mary II of England collapsed. Flashes of pain ran through her head and down her back. She sometimes felt chilly, which caused her to shiver. At other times she sweated. Hundreds of people in London were coming down with a deadly disease called smallpox. A historian at the time wrote, "Smallpox was always present, filling the churchyard with corpses." Queen Mary was afraid she had come down with smallpox. She shut herself in her room at Kensington Palace. She did not want the disease to spread.

Three days later a reddish-purple colour spread across Mary's face. Nine doctors gathered by her bedside. Based on Mary's **symptoms**, they thought the disease could be either measles or smallpox.

symptom change in a person's body or mind that is a sign of a disease

Measles is an infection that causes people to break out in a rash. Doctors hoped the disease was measles and not smallpox. Smallpox was deadlier than measles. The doctors had to wait until Mary developed more symptoms to find out which disease she had.

FAST FACT

The smallpox virus spread very easily. People could catch it when a nearby sick person sneezed or coughed. If people breathed the air around an infected person, they could get the virus.

Mary II was queen of England from 1689 to 1694.

The next day blisters formed on Mary's face, arms, hands and feet. The doctors agreed this was smallpox. But they did not know whether Mary had a deadly form of the disease.

Doctors typically tried a few treatments on people with smallpox. One common treatment was wrapping the patient in blankets in a hot room. Doctors thought this would help the patient sweat out the disease. Some doctors tried bloodletting. This involved draining blood out of a patient's body. Historical accounts do not explain the type of treatment Mary received.

Mary's health soon worsened. Her blisters flattened and spread into red sores along her body. The sores turned purple and black. Red rings formed around each one. Later, the sores filled with blood. The queen gasped for breath. She coughed up blood.

Mary had a rare form of smallpox called haemorrhagic smallpox. This was the deadliest type of smallpox. Victims bled from openings in the body. Mary bled from her nose, eyes and skin. She could no longer eat, drink or speak. Eight days after her first symptoms, Mary died.

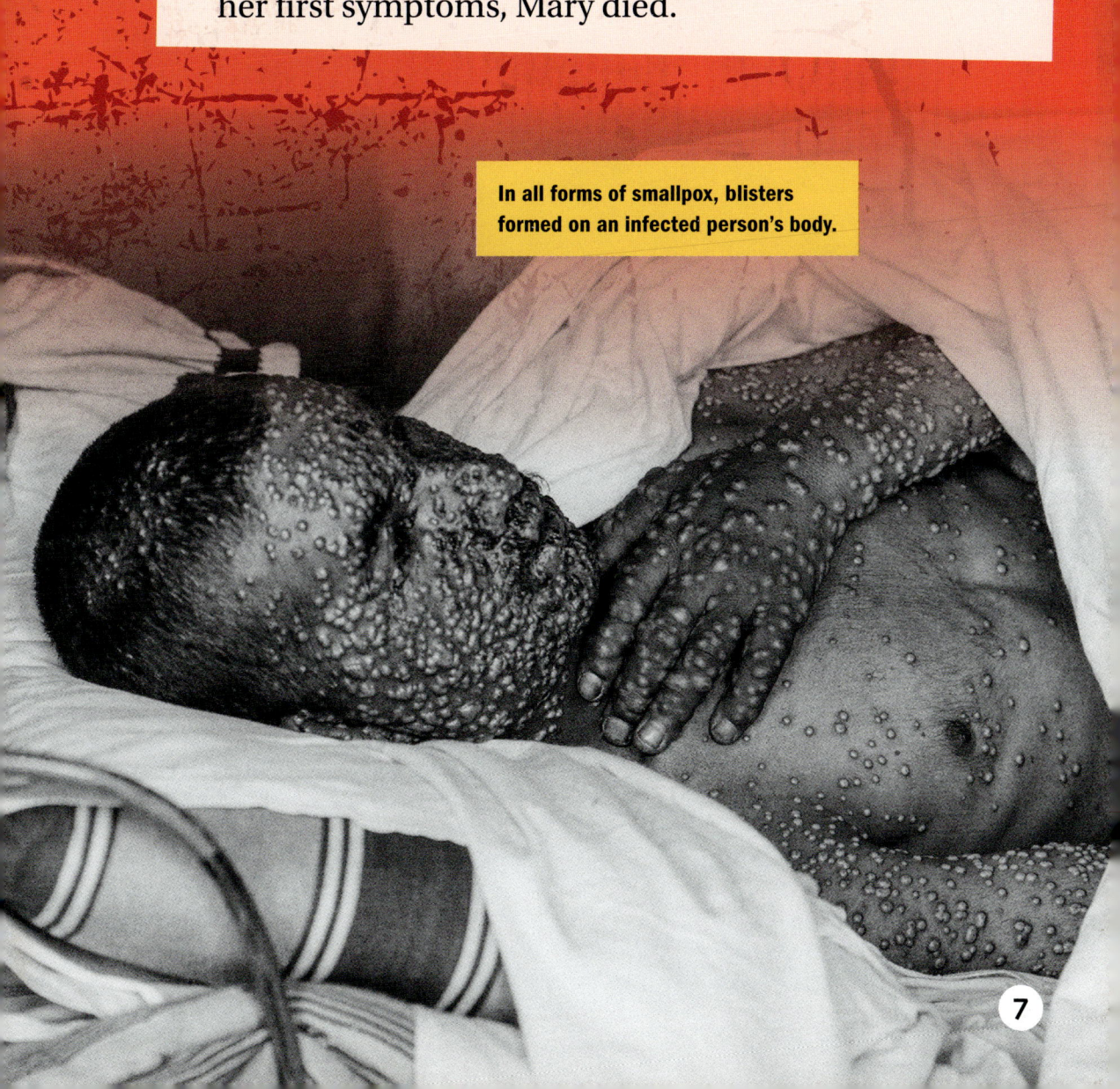

In all forms of smallpox, blisters formed on an infected person's body.

Smallpox often left scars on a person's skin.

WHAT WAS SMALLPOX?

Smallpox was one of the world's deadliest diseases. About three out of every ten people who got it died. Smallpox was **eradicated** worldwide in 1980. But before then the disease had killed hundreds of millions of people.

A **virus** infected people with smallpox. A virus is something that invades a person's body. Once in the body, it attacks a person's cells. The virus then multiplies, causing sickness. Two types of viruses caused smallpox. The variola minor virus caused a mild form of smallpox. People who caught this virus would usually have fevers, headaches and backaches. They would develop rashes. Later bumps called lesions would break out on their skin. The infected person would usually recover within a few weeks. Only about 1 per cent of people died from this type of smallpox.

eradicate completely remove something such as a disease
virus germ that can only grow and reproduce inside the living cells of other organisms

The variola major virus was deadlier and more common than the variola minor virus. Its symptoms included fevers, headaches, backaches and vomiting. A rash developed about four days after the first symptoms. Then the victim's skin would break out in lesions. The lesions would turn into blisters. About 30 per cent of infected people died from this type of smallpox. People usually died 10 to 16 days after their symptoms first appeared. Haemorrhagic smallpox was a type of variola major smallpox. People with haemorrhagic smallpox often died five or six days after getting a rash.

FAST FACT

Another name for smallpox was "the speckled monster". This is because it covered a person's body in blisters and sores.

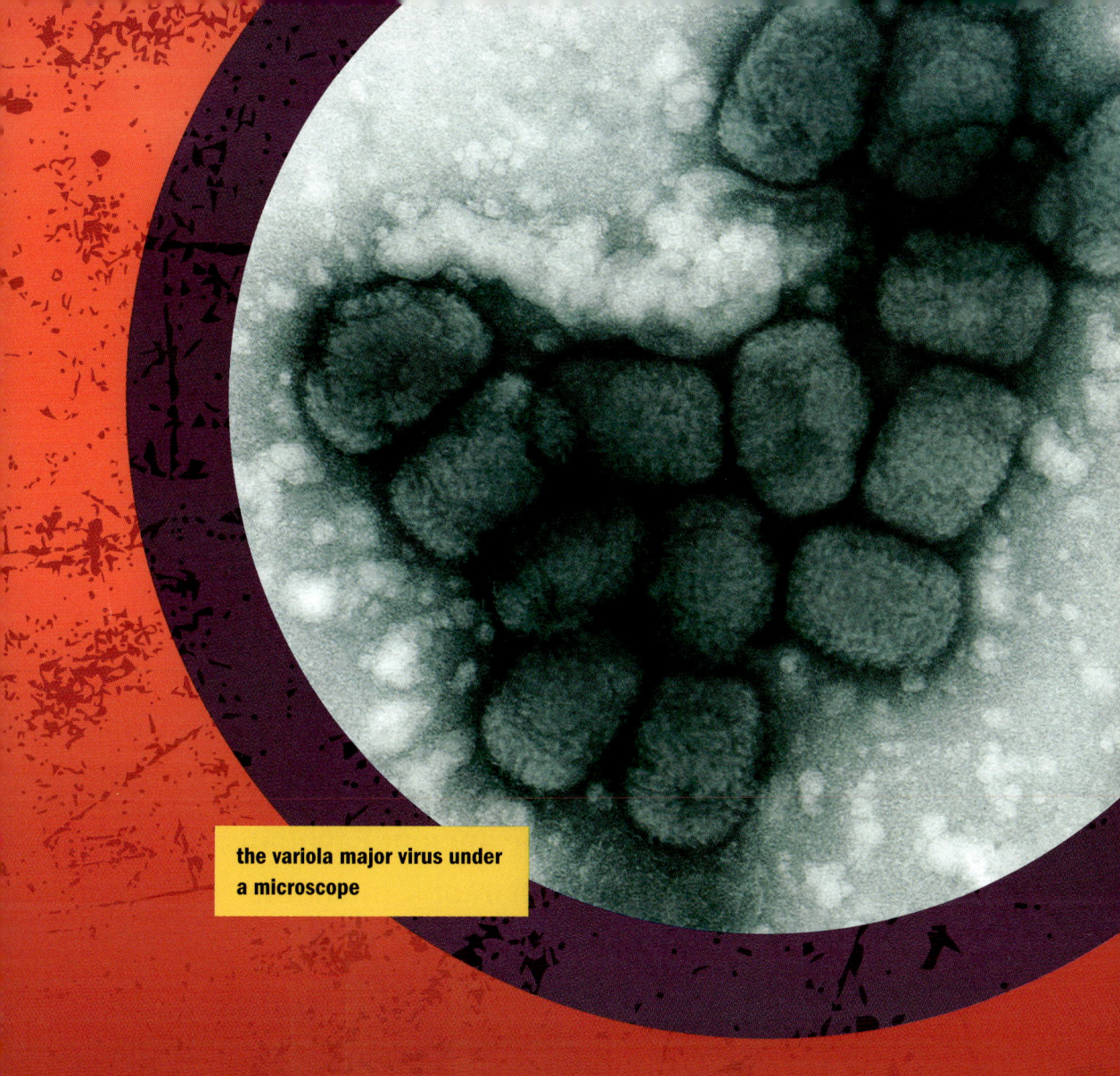

the variola major virus under a microscope

People who survived smallpox had permanent damage. They had pockmarks on their skin. These were scars that disfigured a person's skin. Some people even went blind.

THE HISTORY OF SMALLPOX

Historians believe the first smallpox **epidemic** occurred in Egypt in 1350 BC. Historians are not sure how many people died from this epidemic. Some people think the Egyptian pharaoh Ramses V died of smallpox in 1157 BC. The ancient Egyptians preserved the bodies of their pharaohs, including Ramses V. Scars on Ramses V's face are still visible today. They look like smallpox scars.

FAST FACT
Groups who had not been exposed to smallpox were far more likely to die from it. Their bodies did not know how to fight off the illness.

epidemic outbreak of a disease that affects many people within a particular region

THE SMALLPOX PANDEMIC

Smallpox spread around the world for thousands of years. When a disease spreads all over the world, it is called a **pandemic**. By AD 1000 only a few regions had not been infected by smallpox. It had not spread to Russia, Scandinavia, Iceland, North America or South America. People who lived in infected regions, including Europeans, developed some resistance to the virus.

Pharaoh Ramses V may have died from smallpox.

pandemic outbreak of a disease that spreads across several countries or continents and affects many people

European settlers brought the disease to the unaffected regions. People in these regions had never been exposed to smallpox. This meant that their bodies did not know how to fight the virus.

In 1241, a Danish ship brought smallpox to Iceland. The disease killed nearly half of the country's population. In April 1520, a slave from Africa being held captive on a Spanish ship came down with smallpox. The ship docked in Mexico, and the virus spread throughout the country. About 90 per cent of Mexico's population died from smallpox.

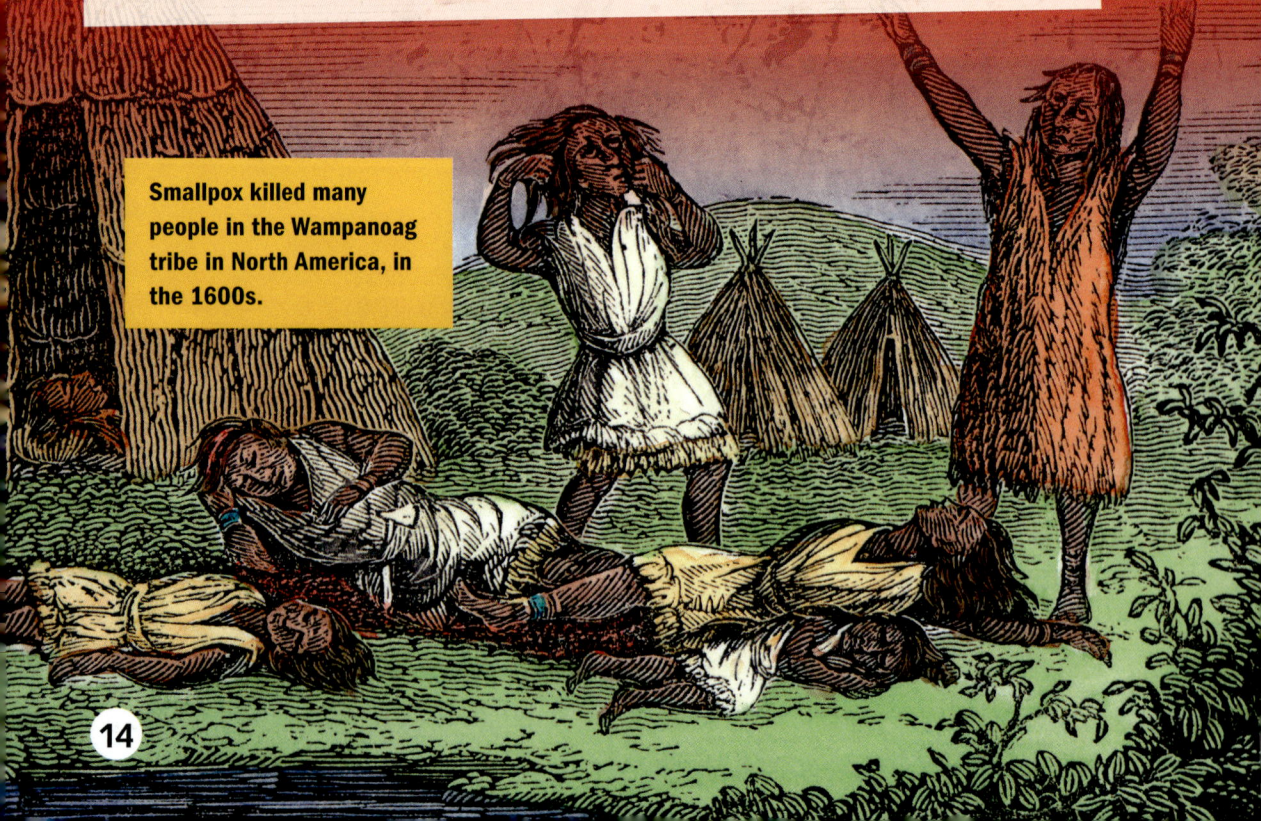

Smallpox killed many people in the Wampanoag tribe in North America, in the 1600s.

SMALLPOX IN NORTH AMERICA

In the 1600s, Dutch, English and French settlers built **colonies** in North America. They also brought smallpox to the region. Thousands of Native Americans died from smallpox. The disease almost wiped out the Algonquin and Narragansett tribes in 1616. Settlers travelled in North America to trade goods, spreading smallpox throughout the region. In 1639, the disease killed about half of the 20,000 members of the Huron-Wendat community.

RED TREATMENT

The colour red was once thought to have special healing powers. It was used to treat smallpox patients, beginning in the 1200s. People who had smallpox slept in red bedsheets and wore red nightclothes. They thought the red cloth would warm their skin so they could sweat out the infection. In the early 1900s, a Danish doctor used red lights to try to heal smallpox patients. He called it the "red treatment". He shone the light on smallpox patients. The red treatment did not work, but doctors kept using this treatment until 1920.

colony   area controlled by another country

CHAPTER 3

SMALLPOX EXPERIMENTS

Early in the disease's history, people began to notice that no one got smallpox twice. In about 1550, Chinese doctors used this knowledge to try to fight smallpox. They crushed smallpox scabs into a powder. Then they blew the powder up a patient's nose. The patient would get a mild form of smallpox but usually recovered. This method was called **variolation**. People in China, Arabia and Africa began to use this method.

LADY MONTAGU

Many doctors in Europe thought variolation was a crazy idea. But an English woman called Lady Mary Wortley Montagu changed their minds. In 1721, an outbreak of smallpox struck London.

variolation method of giving someone smallpox to prevent them from getting the disease a second time

FAST FACT

For a long time, there were many useless treatments for smallpox. One was to feed the patient lentils. Another common treatment was to draw blood from the patient.

Montagu had visited the city of Constantinople in present-day Istanbul, Turkey. She saw doctors variolating people there. She asked her doctor, Charles Maitland, to variolate her son and daughter. Maitland was not against variolation, so he did as she asked. Montagu's children did not come down with smallpox. This persuaded more doctors in Europe to try variolation.

People built hospitals to treat smallpox victims in the 1700s and 1800s.

A BOSTON EXPERIMENT

In 1721, a smallpox epidemic broke out in Boston, Massachusetts, USA. A preacher called Cotton Mather urged doctors to try variolation. Mather had heard about variolation from an African slave called Onesimus. He had seen how variolation could help prevent smallpox.

Mather persuaded a doctor called Zabdiel Boylston to test the variolation method. Boylston used blister fluid from mild cases of smallpox to infect 281 patients. He placed the blister fluid on cuts on his patients' skin. Six of these patients died. The rest recovered. They did not get smallpox a second time.

FAST FACT

People who were infected by smallpox were kept apart from healthy people. This was to help stop the disease spreading.

About 5,980 people got smallpox during the epidemic in Boston. Of those infected, 844 died. Variolation helped saved some people's lives.

A FAILED INVASION

In 1779, smallpox saved England from being invaded. A fleet of French and Spanish ships gathered in the English Channel. They prepared to attack England. The French fleet was made up of about 400,000 men. An outbreak of smallpox struck soldiers on board the French ships. More than half of the men came down with the disease. Hundreds died. The Spanish and French troops did not have enough men to attack. They were forced to retreat.

Cotton Mather supported the variolation method to prevent smallpox.

CHAPTER 4

DEVELOPING A VACCINE

Doctors continued to study smallpox throughout the 1700s. Edward Jenner was an English doctor in the late 1700s. He once heard a milkmaid say, "I shall never have smallpox for I have had cowpox." Cowpox is a mild illness that sometimes affects cows. The disease is related to smallpox but is not deadly. Infected cows develop sores on their udders. The sores are full of **pus**. But the cows tend to recover quickly.

Milkmaids often caught cowpox when they milked infected cows. But they did not get smallpox after being infected with cowpox. They believed that cowpox protected them from smallpox. Jenner wanted to study this to prove if it was true.

pus thick, yellowish fluid that is produced when part of a person's or animal's body becomes infected

A statue in London honours doctor Edward Jenner, who developed the smallpox vaccine in the late 1700s.

COWPOX EXPERIMENTS

In 1796, Jenner treated a milkmaid who had blisters on her hand. Jenner **diagnosed** the blisters as cowpox. He removed some of the pus from the blisters. He then used it to infect an eight-year-old boy called James Phipps. Jenner made two cuts on the boy's arm and rubbed the pus in. James soon came down with cowpox. But he was better within a week. Jenner later tried to give James a mild form of smallpox. But James never got smallpox. This was an important first step in proving that cowpox could help prevent smallpox. It was also the first step in developing a smallpox **vaccine**.

CONTROLLING SMALLPOX

Jenner did more studies. He proved that cowpox protected people from smallpox. This method of using a virus to protect against disease is called vaccination.

diagnose identify a disease from certain symptoms
vaccine substance made up of dead, weakened or living organisms that is injected into a person to protect against a disease

After Jenner published his findings in 1798, the number of vaccinations increased. Vaccination was much safer than variolation. Vaccination had a lower death rate than variolation.

An illustration shows Edward Jenner (centre) vaccinating James Phipps in 1796.

FAST FACT

The root of the word "vaccination" is *vacca*. Vacca is the Latin word for cow.

CHAPTER 5

ELIMINATING SMALLPOX

The smallpox vaccination reduced the number of people who got smallpox. But some people refused to be vaccinated. They thought the vaccination was unsafe.

In March 1947 a few cases of smallpox broke out in New York, USA. Two people died from the disease. The mayor of New York City urged all New Yorkers to get vaccinations. His efforts were successful. About 5 to 6 million people got vaccinations. That was about 64 to 77 per cent of the total population in New York City at the time.

In 1966 the World Health Organization (WHO) began a campaign to eradicate smallpox within 10 years. From 1967 to 1977, WHO teams travelled all over the world to find smallpox cases. They set out to vaccinate 80 per cent of the people in every country. They offered rewards for anyone who reported smallpox cases. When a case was reported, WHO workers separated the patient from healthy people. They vaccinated everyone who had been in contact with the patient. This helped stop the spread of the disease.

An Ethiopian woman receives a smallpox check and vaccination in 1976.

In 1977 a few cases of smallpox broke out in Somalia. After those cases were treated, one year passed without any reported cases. It looked as though the WHO had accomplished its goal.

A NEW TWIST

In 1978 two new cases of smallpox occurred in England. One of the victims was medical photographer Janet Parker. Parker worked at the University of Birmingham.

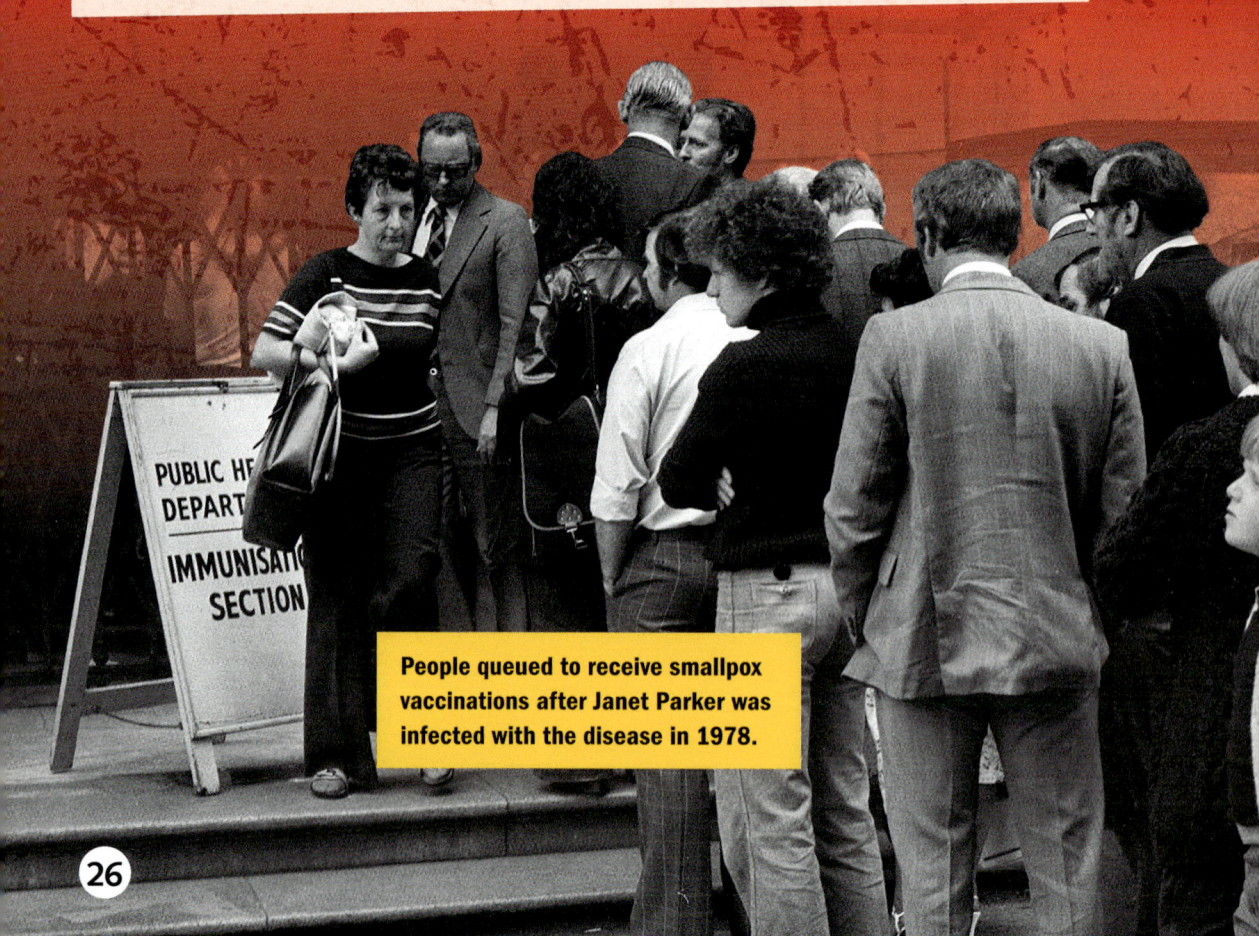

People queued to receive smallpox vaccinations after Janet Parker was infected with the disease in 1978.

A sample of the variola major virus was stored in a laboratory one floor below where Parker worked. Doctors believed the virus moved up an airshaft. Parker probably breathed it in. She also spread the disease to her mother. Parker's mother survived, but Parker did not.

Parker and her mother were the last known victims of smallpox. After Parker's death, the WHO asked all countries to either destroy their smallpox samples or send them to two official WHO locations. These WHO locations were in Georgia, USA, and Moscow, Russia. The samples were locked up in safes. The WHO decided to save these samples until leaders around the world could agree on whether to destroy or save them.

THE SMALLPOX VIRUS TODAY

In May 1980 the WHO made an announcement. The organization said that smallpox had been eradicated. But frozen tubes of the virus are still kept in storage safes around the world. Today the debate continues on whether these tubes should be stored or destroyed. Some scientists think the samples could help researchers learn more about the disease. They think the samples could help people test better smallpox vaccines. Other scientists think the smallpox virus could be used to fight other viruses, such as the human immunodeficiency virus (HIV). But many people think it is too dangerous to keep the samples. They worry that the samples could be stolen and used as a weapon. For now the smallpox virus lives on.

Today only certain people receive the smallpox vaccine, such as members of the US armed forces.

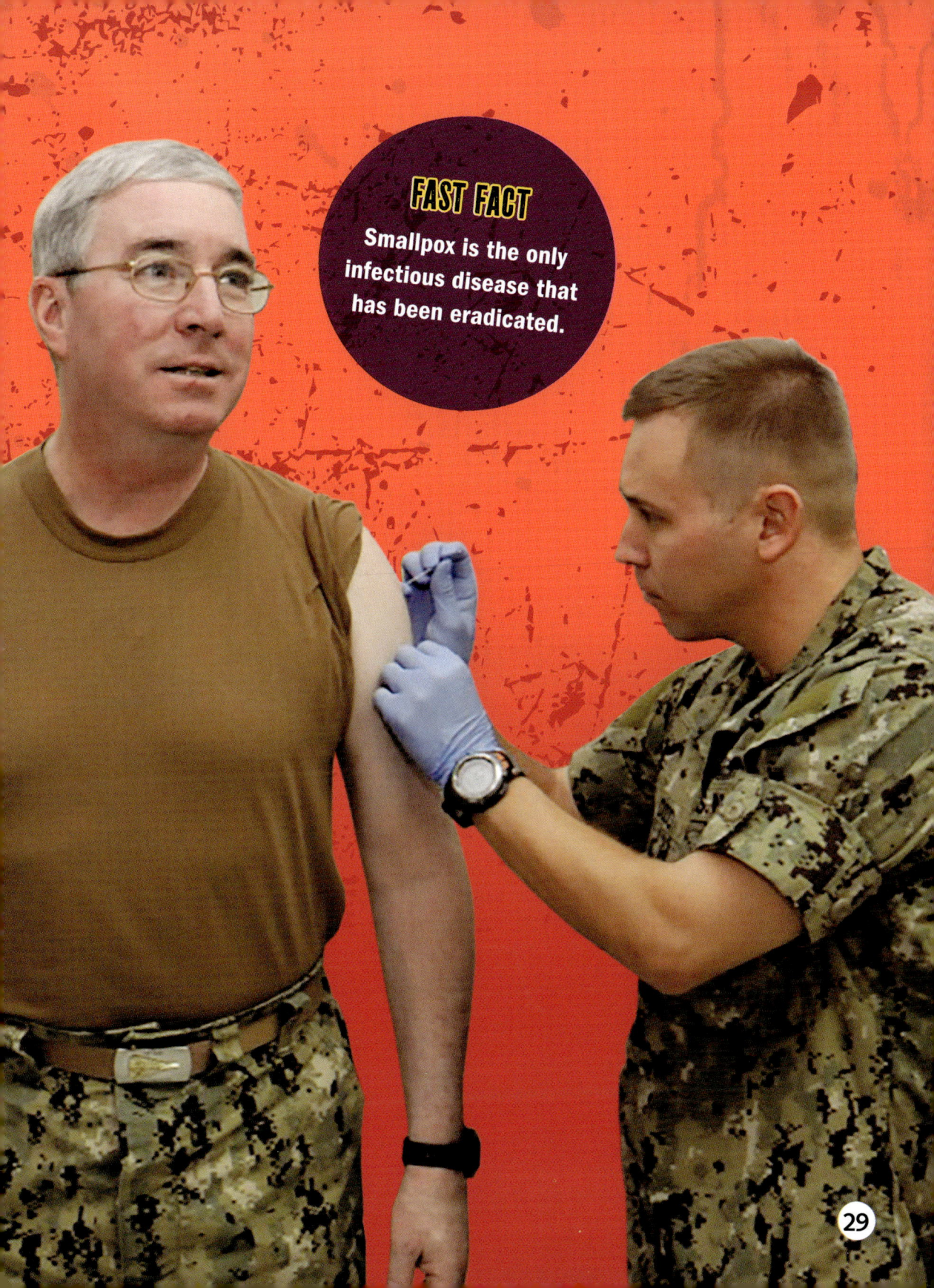

FAST FACT

Smallpox is the only infectious disease that has been eradicated.

GLOSSARY

colony   area controlled by another country

diagnose   identify a disease from certain symptoms

epidemic   outbreak of a disease that affects many people within a particular region

eradicate   completely remove something such as a disease

pandemic   outbreak of a disease that spreads across several countries or continents and affects many people

pus   thick, yellowish fluid that is produced when part of a person's or animal's body becomes infected

symptom   change in a person's body or mind that is a sign of a disease

vaccine   substance made up of dead, weakened or living organisms that is injected into a person to protect against a disease

variolation   method of giving someone smallpox to prevent them from getting the disease a second time

virus   germ that can only grow and reproduce inside the living cells of other organisms

FIND OUT MORE

BOOKS

Health and Disease: From Birth to Old Age (Your Body for Life), Louise Spilsbury (Raintree, 2013)

Promoting Health, Preventing Disease (The Environment Challenge), Rebecca Vickers (Raintree, 2012)

You Wouldn't Want to Live without Vaccinations! Anne Rooney (Franklin Watts, 2015)

WEBSITE

www.bbc.com/teach/class-clips-video/history-ks1-ks2-edward-jenner/zm8fcqt
Learn more about Edward Jenner and vaccinations.

INDEX